M000237683

NEW VINTAGE FRENCH INTERIORS

This book is dedicated to the family.

NEW VINTAGE FRENCH INTERIORS

Text and Photographs by Sébastien Siraudeau

Flammarion

CONTENTS

9 INTRODUCTION

11 A RETREAT IN PROVENCE
Living indoors and out   22

27 SOUTHERN LIVING
Assembling an art collection   42

47 ALONG THE RIVER
Landscaping the garden   57

59 CHÂTEAU LIFE
Living in the country (like the old days)   76

79 A STATELY MANOR
Creating vintage interiors   86

95 A HUNTING LODGE
Bringing the décor to life   105

109 BURGUNDIAN SIMPLICITY
Arousing the curiosity of children   122

127 A FORMER GROCERY IN NORMANDY
Camping in style   141

143 A STONE SANCTUARY
Combining color and vintage finds   150

157 A PROVENÇAL FARMHOUSE
Providing a home for an eclectic collection   164

169 A WOODED RETREAT
Transforming a hoard into an antiques shop   180

185 A HALF-TIMBERED HIDEAWAY
Working from home   198

204 ACKNOWLEDGMENTS

C oming home. It's a return to your origins, a safe haven and a space where you can be secure with your friends and family. It's a private retreat, but also a place to be shared with close companions and others who are just passing through. The derivation of *maison*, the French word for "house," is telling. Instead of using the Latin word for house (*casa*) as its base, it reflects the subtler implications of the Latin verb *manere*, used to express the act of staying in a place, or stopping to rest. Such is the origin of the French word that designates this living space. It may be a Provençal *mas*, a *longère* in Normandy or Brittany, a manor, a farmhouse, an inn, a château, a grand *hôtel particulier*, or a simple country dwelling. It may be small or spacious. It may be an everyday residence, a vacation retreat, or a dream house of the future. The range of possibilities is an inspiration in itself. The important thing is feeling at home and at ease. On your quest to find this perfect destination, you'll tirelessly search, visit, stay, and explore. You'll peer through windows, open the shutters a little, and let the light pour in. Unexpectedly falling in love, you'll retain the best elements: the architecture, the walls. You might alter the space—enlarge it perhaps, or renovate the kitchen and the bedrooms. Sometimes all that's needed is a coat of paint. But, to get things just right, you'll have to perfect the décor as well. Furnish it your own way, hunt for antiques in a range of styles. And the garden, where living spaces open out into nature, shouldn't be neglected either. Plant flowers, cultivate a kitchen garden, construct a terrace, build a shed to potter in, or perhaps even a studio for work. Now you're ready to share and entertain. Welcome to our home!

A RETREAT IN PROVENCE

The location is very remote, tucked away in a hidden valley. Here, Un Mas à Ménerbes—a traditional Provençal farmhouse—sits within close distance of the Petit Lubéron mountain range. It's Jean-Pierre's country retreat; he loves his second home for the brief escapes that take him far from the daily hustle and bustle of Parisian life. He just has to hop on the superfast intercity rail line to get to Avignon, where Jean-Pierre's vacation vehicle will be waiting—a handy little Smart car, perfect for transporting carefree guests and their luggage. A few miles out of the city, the horizon is dotted with villages perched on the mountainsides of central Provence. Gordes, Lacoste, Ménerbes: signposts point the way to the destination. The road runs through vineyards, affording a glimpse of the proud cypresses on the luxurious hotel property of La Bastide de Marie. It twists past glades of holm oaks. Swerving around the last vertiginous curve, Jean-Pierre takes a rocky track through a landscape that becomes a little eerie, almost lunar. The last vestiges of a deserted village are almost lost in the uncultivated scrubland. The *mas* is barely visible. There's just a glimpse of a heavy roof built of roman tiles in shades of brown and orange. The car comes to a stop. A path covered with rough boards threads its way through the wild grasses to the terrace, which is sheltered beneath a vast shady arbor. Although we sense the aftermath of a storm, the air is soft and sweet. Every time he arrives here, Jean-Pierre experiences mingled sensations of disorientation, discovery, and recognition. It's a feeling he loves to share with visitors who feel, as he does, the inexpressible pleasure of "coming home."

The *mas* was restored stone by stone and was finished with simple, sturdy materials (wood, steel, and concrete). The restrained décor is based on several iconic pieces, including Poul Henningsen's PH Artichoke pendant light fixture and Jacobsen chairs discovered in Cube Rouge in Paris. The double-height living room gives access to bedrooms on the ground floor and second level and opens onto an enclosed courtyard that overlooks a valley planted with holm oaks.

The rural, agricultural heritage of the *mas* is evident in rooms that have retained their original dimensions. The walls are all whitewashed to set off the rusticity of the materials used in the furnishings. A few pieces of furniture were found in antiques stores, and the owners have added paintings and sculptures by selected artists. Most of the furniture was custom-made from raw wood and lacquered material that evokes the very geometric, graphic look of the 1950s.

LIVING INDOORS AND OUT

The *mas* is two hundred years old, and the historic structure has been preserved; only the woodwork was redesigned by an architect. A few windows were pierced in the thick walls to provide natural light for the interior. Living spaces open onto a courtyard, which overlooks the valley through a heavy double door made of red cedar. Down the hill, the owner has restored the *borie* — a simple hut once used to shelter local shepherds — and has added a spacious terrace suspended above the valley (pages 24–25). Jean-Pierre, a designer for the firm Modderne, has selected just the right pieces from here and there, including an outdoor canopy bed, a fanciful windmill, and a long table suitable for hosting convivial summer dinners.

SOUTHERN LIVING

Constructed mostly during the eighteenth century on medieval foundations, this spacious residence has the distinctive presence of a grand home that has escaped the depredations of ephemeral styles and trends. Built between the ancient ramparts of the small fortified village of Les Beaumettes and the dry-stone walls of a terraced garden—known locally as a *jardin en restanques*—its tall ocher facade that faces the road is covered with lush Virginia creeper. Behind faded shutters, a labyrinthine interior evokes the great events of the building's past and its noble residents, who included a Seigneur de Balma in the Middle Ages and Baron Autric de Vintimille in the early days of the French Revolution. Vaulted ceilings, a spiral staircase crafted from stone, and traditional hexagonal tiled floors all attest to this distinguished past. The contemporary décor draws on folk art and traditional handicrafts, as well as vintage design, carrying on the vital spirit of the home, which is now a country guesthouse. In large part the creation of Thierry and Serge (who lived life in the slow lane here for almost fifteen years), it has recently been sold to Michelle and Sylvain. Formerly viticulturists in the Sancerre region, the couple were captivated by the house and the village's streets and people. They were also attracted to the pleasures of life in this picturesque Provençal setting, which seems to have escaped the ravages of time and encourages a surprisingly carefree existence. Hosts and guests relish the time they spend in this house, so aptly named Au Ralenti du Lierre, after the "slow-motion" growth of its signature ivy covering.

The kitchen opens onto the terrace, where Mallet-Stevens chairs flank an old faience stove. The storage cabinets are simply covered with recycled aged window blinds. Two antique faucet fixtures, similar to those in the Château de Fontainebleau, are installed above the double marble sink. On the table, Serge has fashioned a whimsical still life using old-fashioned cooking molds.

Echoing the arching curves of the interior vaults, an Arco
de Castiglioni floor lamp lights the dining-room table,
whose finish has been stripped down to expose the wood
beneath. It is surrounded by 1950s chairs in black steel
and textured Skaï leatherette, which were once used
on the set of Jacques Tati's film *Mon Oncle*.

The pages of an old Bourgeois pastel color chart inspired the selection of tones for the walls and paneled bases painted in trompe l'oeil in one of the bedrooms. In the sitting room, a Valentine paint display case has been repurposed for exhibiting sculptures.

A bedroom is tucked away beneath the roof, whose
heavy beams are painted soft blue, complementing
the rough surface of the terra-cotta jar and the
mellow patina of the walls and the door.

ASSEMBLING AN ART COLLECTION

When you live in Provence, especially in a large house, you're bound to be a collector. It's both fun and necessary to furnish the place, but beyond that you may experience the desire—and need—to be creative. Serge took his time finding his own inspiration at Au Ralenti du Lierre. He set up a workshop beneath the stone vaults and packed it with a vast store of seemingly random objects and articles: pieces of metalwork, wood, and scratched plaster; piles of eighteenth-century decorative elements, massed together to create a sculpture reminiscent of a forest. He meticulously assembles, welds, and polishes industrial components to reveal strange and evocative creatures. A piece from a foundry becomes a spectral totem. Fuel tanks of legendary Terrot motorbikes metamorphose into benches resembling mutant sea creatures. Some of these works, in a state of small-scale controlled chaos, are still on display in the house. Serge is now exhibiting in a new gallery that he has just opened in Lyon, aptly named La Galerie du Désordre.

ALONG THE RIVER

A pair of oars, a straw basket, and a Panama hat. Yannick has assembled everything he needs for his favorite pastime: boating on the Loire, which flows past the bottom of his garden. Cradled above the restless river, Le Clos des Trémières—named for the hollyhocks that abound in its garden—is adjacent to the hillside village of Montsoreau. On the foundations of an old winery, Yannick and his wife Hélène initially designed a weekend retreat that also served as a small boutique for Yannick, who is an antiques dealer. Hélène, an architect, drew inspiration from old postcards to design a house with rooms of varying sizes on several levels. Constructed naturally from white tufa—the stone extracted from ancient quarries along the banks of the Loire—the house fits perfectly into the pastoral village that lies beneath the famous château. On the main floor, the living room is laid out with a row of windows that are open to the river's reflected light. Attuned to the changing hues of the countryside, the interior features pale colors: seashore blue, anise green, linen white, and chocolate brown. The house boasts mementoes with sentimental value and other cherished objects, including a seventeenth-century statue of Saint Nicholas. But the overall décor derives its personality from a skillful blend of styles and periods, ranging from Gustavian Swedish to contemporary, reflecting the artfully melded tastes of an antiquarian and an architect. But nothing is set in stone. Between the Montsoreau flea market, held every month on the far side of the village, and trips that range from the Île de Ré to the Swedish coast, Hélène and Yannick might just make a few additional changes.

A broad band of blue has been painted on the lower
portion of the whitewashed walls. Contemporary
furniture mingles comfortably with antiques. The
dresser and Louis XVI armchair, reupholstered in
vintage hemp cloth, are painted grayish-beige
in the Swedish style.

The interior of the dresser in the sitting room is painted the same tone as the lower portion of the walls. It houses several sets of glasses, silverware, and an elegant array of tableware from the Régence and Victor collections made by Astier de Villatte.

Covered with an aged hemp cloth runner, the outdoor
table is set with antique tableware. It overlooks the
river where a small boat makes its way to the landing
stage in Montsoreau.

LANDSCAPING THE GARDEN

Built against a hillside, the garden of Le Clos des Trémières is constructed on several levels, like the gardens terraced with dry-stone walls (*jardins en restanques*) in the south of France. Within these walls, bordered by hordes of hollyhocks (they thrive in calcareous soil), the antiquarian demonstrates his love of both flowers and beautiful objects. An ancient wall has been rebuilt with multiple niches to house cast-iron vases, pots, and decorative bird sculptures fashioned from painted cement. Carved stone objects appear throughout the garden, such as a jardiniere or bench whose designs echo tree bark. A marvelous garden room has been created, incorporating a florist's planter rack decorated with old zinc trim: an ideal spot for a picnic, and to enjoy the pleasures of life on the banks of the Loire.

CHÂTEAU LIFE

L ife is a story. Céline and Pierre's can be traced in their journey from the broad avenues of the Parisian suburbs to the rich farming country of the Beauce region and the wooded valleys of Perche, which lie to the capital's northwest. The current tale is set in a small château built in 1804—a setting worthy of a family saga, at least one that saw their dream of reuniting the whole family come true. Passionate about French heritage, Pierre Génin—who recently undertook the revival of Lum'art, an artisanal lighting firm located in this rural area—studied the history of the house, poring over illustrated texts on the region and studying the land registry, established under Napoléon Bonaparte, in great detail. At the end of an unrelenting treasure hunt, after exploring sites and documentary evidence, he unearthed the true story. Pierre never lets a year or a season go by without revealing another page in this history. Through studying old engravings, he discovered the original perimeter of the park that surrounded the house. He observed the rigorous codes for the geometric layout of a traditional *jardin à la française*, its pools bordered with stately alleyways and its parterres planted with tree roses, making an elegant architectural statement. That will be next in line for restoration. Nature has reasserted her rights there; brambles and ivy climb everywhere, swallowing up the leafy groves and scattered outbuildings, and giving the impression of an ephemeral setting for some romantic tale. Something very similar nourished the fictionalized childhood reminiscences of Marcel Proust, whose country home can be visited nearby.

Céline and Pierre embarked upon a variety of improvements to the interiors, boldly juxtaposing vivid colors and contemporary elements with traditional ones. The pantry, painted an audacious firecracker red, adjoins a small dining room that has soft pastel blue walls. A century-old Godin range sits imposingly upon a floor with checkerboard cement tiles. Lighting is provided by a La Varenne ceiling fixture with a satin nickel finish made by Lum'Art.

All of the furniture in the living and dining rooms has a long family history. This heritage includes the Maison Génin, a furniture maker located on Rue du Faubourg Saint-Antoine—the traditional Parisian furniture-manufacturing district. The porcelain table service was painted by Céline.

The bedrooms are painted in soft, soothing colors—mauve, dusty rose, and pearl gray. The parents selected one of Manuel Canovas's fabrics to cover the Louis XVI sofa, but their daughter Lucie preferred a tweed with a tartan motif in her bedroom. The bathroom's tiled floor and basin on legs are original. The globe-shaped Ombre de Lune ceiling light is by Lum'Art's craftsmen. Valentine makes her own statement by adding a graphic industrial aesthetic touch to another room (pages 72–73).

LIVING IN THE COUNTRY (LIKE THE OLD DAYS)

The domain once had a substantial farmhouse, which is no longer standing. However, it still retains numerous outbuildings and installations that allow its residents to live completely self-sufficiently, due in part to scientific advances and technical adaptations. A water-distribution system allows recovery and storage in cisterns and wells to supply the entire property, which still incorporates a pheasantry, cider mill, washhouse, and fishpond. The windmill, a striking innovation in its time, is an interesting feature. For now the winter garden and greenhouse (pages 74–75) are in use again; Céline is busy experimenting with repotting and collecting cuttings to restore the park's plantings.

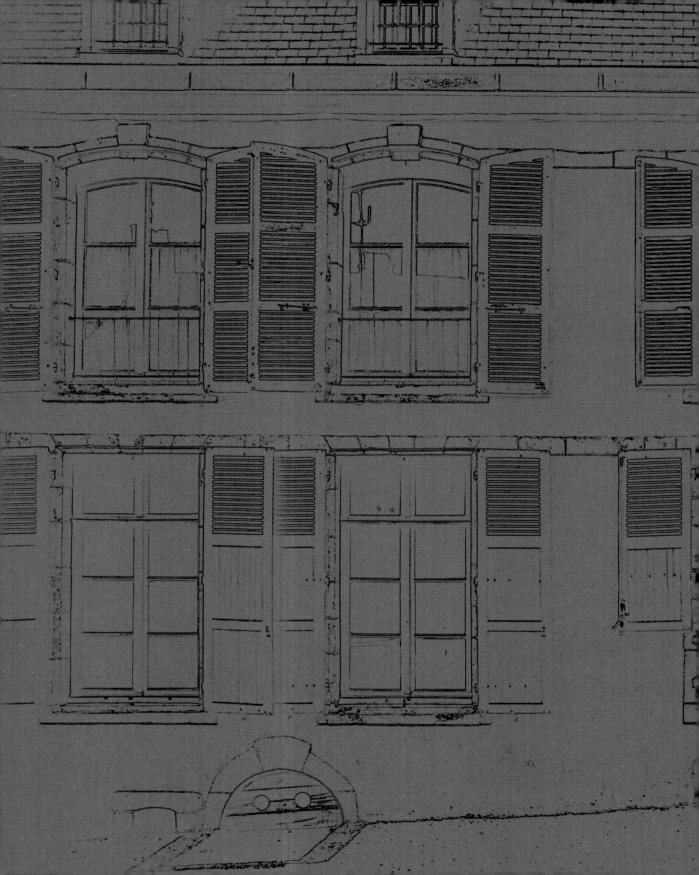

A STATELY MANOR

ellême is an enchanting medieval town in the Perche region. Along with Mortagne, it attracts visitors captivated by picturesque country villages as well as those answering the siren call to return to the land. Set in the heart of a rural landscape, once crossed by the royal road that ran from Paris to Brittany, the walls of Bellême preserve the memories of lords and peasants, merchants and travelers. Narrow lanes lead step by step around the fortified town; shops replete with charm offer all that's needed for gracious living—flowers, collectibles, and intriguing galleries. Everywhere you turn, the facades of the houses rise majestically, austere but elegant, revealing very little of the discreet private lives of the residents within. You might peer through a window, and speculate, imagine, hope. Josiane, along with Joël—a native of the region—embarked on this inquisitive journey, finally crossing the threshold of one of these secret buildings. This stately *hôtel particulier* has borne witness to the passage of centuries and great moments in the history of the Perche region. In all that time, it has had only four owners: country gentlemen or equerries of the king. They are commemorated today by the names of the bedrooms in this unusual guesthouse. Heavy latched doors, a solid oak staircase, traditional hexagonal floor tiles, and monumental fireplaces have all been refurbished in a comprehensive restoration program that has preserved the building's authenticity and dignity. It is a worthy setting for an interior that features treasures collected from many sources, ranging from the sixteenth through the twentieth centuries. The atmosphere is timeless.

The kitchen windows open onto the enclosed garden.
Its walls are simply whitewashed and hung with
Romantic landscapes collected from flea markets.
Some are plain canvases, others framed, like the
transom painting hanging above the fireplace.

CREATING VINTAGE INTERIORS

From the village of Mortagne to Nogent-le-Rotrou, collectors flock to the Perche region to hunt for all sorts of antique finds—from salvaged architectural materials to intriguing curios. The proprietors of the Hôtel de Suhard, experts on the matter, have searched the region's best sources to discover old treasures and whimsical creations. In the living room, the doors and their frames—some unfinished and others sanded down—seem to confront each other as if in a painting. Two inviting sofas stand side by side, facing the marble mantelpiece, in keeping with the room's eighteenth-century sensibility. Old documents, simply rolled up, are tucked beneath a glass dome, and specimens from a herbarium have been mounted in a Napoléon III frame and hung above a blackened commode. Framed or arranged in bouquets, gorgonian coral pieces from antiques dealer Stéphanie Mayeux are transformed into veritable works of art. Elsewhere in the room, ornamental stones are simply placed, as if a collector were just starting on a brand-new project.

On the third floor, a suite named in honor of Mathilde Chazelles—a former owner who died without an heir—is painted a soft powder pink. A traditional wattle and daub partition, deliberately left partially open, separates the main room from the bathroom, which—like all the others in the house—was a recent creation. Pretty wall fixtures crafted by the artist Marie Christophe lend a hint of poetry to the lighting.

A banquette upholstered in mustard-colored linen and
quilted bed headboards give this room an early
nineteenth-century feel. The Chartier des Rieux blue
chosen for the walls lends a nautical touch, which is
cleverly emphasized by the naval officer's simple
gabardine coat, hung on a dressmaker's mannequin.

A HUNTING LODGE

I t's not often one gets carte blanche on a project, so when Grégoire Courtin was given the chance to oversee this one, he accepted the offer without any hesitation. An antiques dealer, collector, and informed lover of cabinets of curiosities, he enjoys sharing his passion for unique objects. Intrigued by Grégoire's eclectic and varied interests (he actually collects projects), a couple who patronized his shop in La Chartre-sur-le-Loir asked him to supervise the restoration and decoration of their newly purchased house. An eighteenth-century hunting lodge, the property is located in a remote area of the Sarthoise countryside in northern France, surrounded by woods and ponds to which wild geese and ducks flock. She is a painter of animal subjects, he is a dedicated hunter. Both love nature and enjoy entertaining. These interests established a framework for the designer. While skilled artisans busied themselves restoring the building from top to bottom with all its authentic details, Grégoire embarked on designing the interior. Visitors enter through the mudroom, a vast paneled hall hung with satchels and oilcloth jackets. A bench runs all around so that the hunters can sit to remove their muddy boots. In the middle of the room stands a large table, intended for game brought back from the hunt, which was made to order by the project's woodworkers. It displays the stuffed head of a boar reposing on a platter. The dining room has two double-shelved drapers' tables, capable of accommodating as many as sixteen guests, who dine beneath the amused gaze of humanized animals painted by their hostess. Peering through the narrow doorway, the visitor catches a glimpse of an antelope's trophy head, and the décor comes alive.

In the kitchen, the designer has aligned a row of
opaline white ceiling fixtures with their traditional
counterweights. In the next room, the long console
tables exhibit trophies and Baroque gilt wood
sculptures, displayed like flaming urn finials.

BRINGING THE DÉCOR TO LIFE

Curled up comfortably in the corner of an armchair lies a fox, its ears pricked up, listening, and one wary eye open. It's on the lookout. The creature's pose seems utterly true to life, but it's actually a stuffed fox. As early as the sixteenth century, taxidermy techniques allowed the preservation of hitherto unknown species encountered on newly explored continents. Scholars, botanists, and naturalists, as well as educated gentlemen, devised the "cabinet of curiosities" to display their jealously guarded treasures. Such unique collections were very much in vogue in the nineteenth century, the era when the legendary taxidermy firm Deyrolle was established. The same spirit of curiosity is being reborn in this house today, spurred by a certain compulsion to collect. The hunter has made the lodge a place to display his own trophies. They have been staged in a skillfully contrived setting, together with other treasures, in a decorative scheme that provides a vivid sense of life.

The original carpentry work is on view in this
guestroom tucked beneath the eaves. All the
woodwork in the bedrooms was custom-made,
including the partition that separates the bedroom
and the bathroom, partially open and finished
with basketwork louvers.

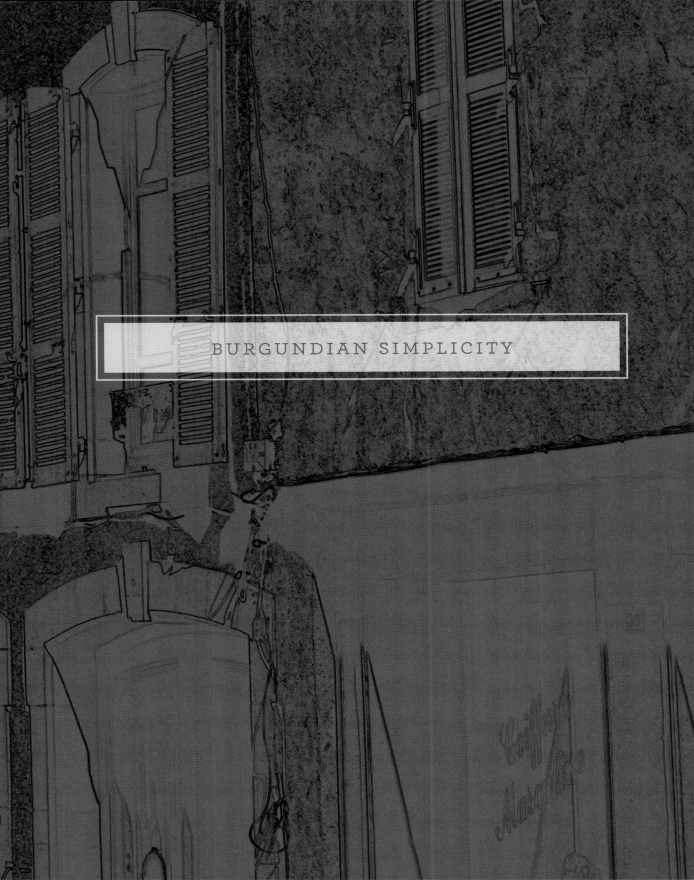

BURGUNDIAN SIMPLICITY

Estaminet *Coquet,* or Quaint Café—Anne Soulier hesitatingly evokes the name of the imaginary universe, with neither walls nor borders, that she created with her blog upon her arrival in her new house. On the pages of her simply illustrated, personal, and unpretentious journal, she shared the wonder of her young children as they grew up in a small town in Burgundy, far from the noise and crowds of the city where they had been born. A flower, a lighted candle, a butterfly, a four-leafed clover—these seemingly trivial details and treasured moments bear witness to the daily delights of family life. Anne recalls that apparently irrational moment when she and Pascal decided—on a complete whim—to move into this spacious residence of over four thousand square feet with some fifteen rooms. The work required was enormous and took more than two years. It was only the blink of an eye in the history of the house, though, which had been in the same family since it was built in 1867. It seemed like an eternity to Anne, who admits she took her time to complete the project. As the seasons went by, Anne and Pascal settled in, deploying gallons of Farrow and Ball paint to add color to the lofty walls of each room. They became avid collectors, imbuing the house and its garden with a spirit of serenity. They got married, made friends with their neighbors, and were content with their life. However, to their own surprise, they have just radically changed course and moved south to the Côte d'Azur. It just proves that Anne loves to turn to the next page—and not only in her journal. She is well aware that you have to close some doors behind you if you're to reinvent yourself elsewhere, in a place where fresh joys await.

The ceilings, with their décor of cornices and stucco
rosettes, the coated walls, and the paneled base
moldings are all painted in a range of subtle pastel
halftones, enhancing the homey elegance of this
unpretentious house.

Everyday meals are served in the pantry, where a
simple bistro table and chairs have been painted a
chaste white. On the walls, a chestnut-wood Enkidoo
apple drying rack designed by Godefroy de Virieu and
a schoolroom poster from the publishing house
Rossignol are all that's needed to complete
the room's décor.

AROUSING THE CURIOSITY OF CHILDREN

Butterflies under a glass cloche, artificial mushrooms, a basket of hazelnuts and chestnuts, and a squirrel: Pauline and Gaspard, the children of the house, have created their own little cabinet of curiosities. The exhibits have been gleaned from secondhand shops and garage sales—Burgundy is full of them—or from strolls through the forests that line the roads of the mountainous Morvan region, or simply while wandering around their own garden. Country life sharpens a child's appetite for exploration. Like naturalists and explorers of bygone centuries, by perusing books and encyclopedias, such as this illustrated *Inventaire des Fruits et Légumes* (Inventory of Fruits and Vegetables, page 121), they learn to decipher the world around them, picking out stories that have a poetry of their own. Maybe Gaspard will one day grow up to be an archeologist himself.

The original wood floors seem to be straight out of
Gustave Caillebotte's painting *The Floor Planers*
(1875). In this case, however, there's no laborious
scraping going on—it's just young Gaspard playing in
this spacious playroom.

A FORMER GROCERY IN NORMANDY

Four walls and a roof. Nothing could ever be that simple for Karine and François, whom you'll meet at L'Épicerie du Pape (The Pope's Grocery Store). But wait. It's not a grocery store any more. They've converted an old village shop into their home and made it an inviting bed-and-breakfast establishment. Le Pape? We're not referring to the Holy Father. That's the botanical term you'd have to know to learn that Karine is fond of the colors of the flowering plant lunaria (honesty), best known in France as *monnaie-du-pape* (the pope's coins). That's where their story begins: with four walls, a roof, a flower garden, and the countless tiny details that enrich life in this Norman farmhouse. Inside, you'll find workmen's lunch pails hanging in the kitchen, a megaphone from a freight ship, a sailor's cap, a Velosolex moped, a collection of multicolored siphons, a seat from a movie theater, a giant stuffed toy version of ET, and a landscape of the cliffs in the Caux region overlooking the coast of upper Normandy; the pope's family loves to go antique-hunting. There are three dogs, four cats, and even a horse for Nina; the pope's family loves animals. There's a fire in the hearth, a big, beautifully set table, and beds that are always made up with embroidered sheets; the pope's family loves to entertain. There's a cabin and a holiday caravan in the garden: the pope's family loves to travel. The family is always intent on a new project; they always have some new mission in mind. Perhaps they'll fix up an old car, experiment with "glamping," or move south to the Lubéron for a change. Or maybe they'll just stay at home, safe in their family cocoon.

Originally a one-story dwelling, the farmhouse was
enlarged with new extensions. Partitions were
removed to create a generously sized living area,
accommodating an antique convent table around
which friends can gather.

A display rack originally for seed packs now holds visiting cards and old photos of the pope's family. Insatiable and imaginative antique hunters, Karine and François track down fresh ideas from dealers ranging from Atelier 42 to L'Empreinte, which have set up shop in Lyons-la-Forêt. François loves old mechanical devices and marine memorabilia—he's done a lot of sailing. Karine has amassed an impressive collection of faience and porcelain Virgins; they once occupied an honored place as benign protectors of local households.

The guesthouse rooms are sometimes used by friends
who are passing through. Many of them share their
hosts Karine and François's appreciation
for the simple things in life.

CAMPING IN STYLE

François has designed a cabin that's really a complete little house at the far end of the garden. It has four walls and a roof, everything required for stay-at-home vacations. Inspired by Swedish mountain huts, the exterior is red-painted wood, and the interior is pure white. It's completely set apart—used as guest quarters—and is heated with a vintage Ankarsrum wood-burning Viking mini-stove dating from the 1940s. The light-filled interior includes the essentials for comfortable living: a swimming-pool clothes rack, soft bedding with an eiderdown quilt by Bord de Scène, a metal basin with faucets for shared use, and a cow trough converted into a shower stall. During the summer months, the authentic 1960s Eriba Puck Touring Caravan, "the queen of mobile travel," is a playhouse for the children—unless it's hitched up to the Fiat 500, ready to hit the road!

A STONE SANCTUARY

Meadows filled with sunflowers, fields of golden wheat, the allure of summer nights—when the door to this old stone house swings open, images of carefree days spring to mind. They are spontaneous memories, like the fragments of vivid colors you see in a kaleidoscope, Polaroid snapshots in a treasured album, or the daydreams of an eternally youthful girl. Micheline is the loving mother of five (grown-up) daughters, but she's as tireless as ever when it comes to imagining, transforming, and inventing. Her guesthouse is a playground, a breeding ground for self-expression. It sits high up on the hillside of Barjac, close to the château and manse, as if contemplating the Ardèche and the Cevennes plateau. Built during the Renaissance, the structure is almost invisible from the village's maze of sun-drenched lanes. It has retained its thick walls, tall windows, and ribbed vaults, but Micheline has restored the house herself from top to bottom and never tires of adding new touches. With a background in fine arts, she loves exploring all sorts of materials, colors, and objects. This doesn't involve many new purchases—it's a matter of hunting down antiques, recycling, being creative and a do-it-yourselfer, all exercised with determination and unquenchable enthusiasm. To inspire your own spirit of creativity, just listen to Micheline, who'll gladly share her practical expertise and innovative ideas in her studio on the ground floor. If you want to search for antiques, you just have to walk out the door, because Barjac is host to one of the most delightful antique fairs in the south of France. Take the opportunity to visit when the sunflowers are in bloom, and savor the sense of freedom.

Fresh from the fields, sunflowers bring brilliant color
to create cheerful displays, such as these still lifes
propped up behind a decorative fiberglass tray.
Micheline's papier-mâché ceiling light in the entry hall
was inspired by Italian Cupolone suspension lamps.

à table ...

COMBINING COLOR AND VINTAGE FINDS

Les Nomades Baroques, Micheline's whimsically named guesthouse, is a worthy pretext for creative and recreational playfulness. While working on the basic requirements of the restoration, she added exuberant expressions of color and graphic design. There's just as much color in the furniture as on the walls. Micheline does all of her painting using pigments, mostly purchased from Établissements Chauvin, which is located in the rugged ocher countryside of the "Provençal Colorado." Combined with a lime or Blancolor base, sometimes with the addition of a fixative for walls and halls, the pigments allow her to create unique and carefully selected colors. Hence the lime green applied to the frame of an armchair. It's a shade that obsesses Micheline and she uses it often; you'll even find it on the Skaï leatherette upholstery of a pair of Charles Eames aluminum office chairs dating from the 1970s.

In the bedroom known as "Les Locataires" (The
Tenants), orange accents punctuate the predominantly
khaki-green décor. Shades of this latter color are used
on the bed headboard, which is fashioned from solid
wood construction boards, and a green band painted
along the wall suggests a horizon line.

A PROVENÇAL FARMHOUSE

anon loves her house. Manon loves houses in general. She loves them for the stories they tell and the stories they inspire. Her working life is divided between town and travel, but she rediscovers a sense of peace during the summer days she spends at her house in Saint-Rémy-de-Provence. A little bridge spans the Canal des Alpilles, and the track passes one garden after another until it reaches this blissful retreat, a picturesque old farmhouse. Manon has preserved its sun-drenched facade, its timeless blue shutters, its vines, and its shaded arbor. Her closest neighbor was born here. This elderly lady still recalls the old stone kitchen sink and her grandmother's daily tasks; she lived here amid the drone of the cicadas and the fragrances of Provence so beloved by the local poet Frédéric Mistral. Although she enjoys poetry, as well as Maurice Pagnol's cinematic works, this Manon is not the heroine of Pagnol's *Manon des Sources*. Her real name is Chantal. Her grandson nicknamed her Manon, and when it came to finding a title for her blog, that's the name she chose. The stories she's been recounting for several years now are full of details, anecdotes, encounters, insights, and photos of her house, her creations, and her innumerable collections. A former professional fashion stylist, Manon retains her gift for composition, arrangements, colors, and sewing. She loves old fabrics and linens, embroidered or plain; she snips, stitches, and transforms them in her leisure time. Manon also takes pleasure in entertaining guests. In honor of today's visitors, she's baked a delectable chiffon cake. She has time enough for everything.

Manon has left the imperfections in the floor and walls
undisturbed in order to retain the authenticity of the
house. Thoughtfully collected objects attest to her loving
care for the home. On the mantelpiece, an old wooden
horse stands next to a set of wooden ninepins.

PROVIDING A HOME FOR AN ECLECTIC COLLECTION

For Manon, any old excuse will do to go hunting for antiques. There are real treasures to be found everywhere, from the villages of Provence to the city of Lyon, especially at Florence Bouvier's stand in the flea market that's held along the canal. Manon used to accompany her father on such expeditions, and she has a passion for collecting in her blood. Even as a little girl, she had a hoard of flower-patterned milk jugs. Her country home has become a welcoming repository for her many collections, presented in no particular order. You'll find straw cowboy hats, stacks of scented soaps from Marseille, and empty frames propped up against the courtyard wall (pages 166–67). Manon has transformed the corridor into a giant mood board. This collage of paintings found at flea markets forms a creative wall reminiscent of virtual interfaces such as Pinterest or Tumblr.

A WOODED RETREAT

F inding my way through the morning mist in my Volvo, I take a fork in the road and suddenly enter a wood teeming with wildlife. At a tiny crossroads in a place known as Le Breuil, I come to a welcome halt. Olivier's little house is tucked away amid dense undergrowth and grassy meadows, immersed in nature. Somewhere, a donkey brays. A lover of flowers and knowledgeable about trees, Olivier was determined to find a house with a garden he could enjoy. He wanted a property that was somewhat secluded, but not too remote from village activities, because he also enjoys urban life. Olivier is a writer, and it was one of his editor friends who helped him find this retreat after exploring the byways of this area of countryside situated less than two hours from Paris. He had fond memories of the garden of his childhood that his father lovingly cultivated around his home in Marne-la-Coquette. Le Breuil has become his current source of inspiration. Olivier indulges all his passions here. In the house he writes, obviously. In the garden, he's become a landscape artist, constructing banks, planting heather, pruning fruit trees, and experimenting with the art of topiary. In the nearby gatehouse, he assembled a veritable stockpile of flea-market finds, eventually opening a shop. You might find a few gardening implements, a Napoléon III armchair, stuffed wildfowl, birdcages, cement mushroom garden sculptures, and a gnome awaiting your arrival. Depending on the season, Olivier brings together objects that appeal to him for his own garden, and for anyone else's. His enthusiasm never flags, and he's very willing and able to design for others, creating a garden where everyone can feel at ease. Just like home.

Vintage garden tools hang on interior walls painted in
Pea Green by Farrow and Ball, the firm whose paints
are so prized by the British. The Chesterfield and red
velvet sofa in the library are perfect partners for
afternoons pleasurably spent reading
or in conversation.

COMPTE DEPÔT DE FONDS
COUVREMENTS TOUTES OPÉRATIONS
AUX ÉLEVEURS SUR TITRES
ET AUX HERBAGERS PAIEMENT DES COUPONS
AUX

Echoing the region's agricultural history, an old
signboard from the traditional livestock fairs,
uncovered by Olivier at La Maison Fassier,
hangs in the entry hall.

Among his other curiosities, Olivier keeps
birds' nests he has collected from his garden
in a little glass casket, next to which stands a
disapproving stuffed goose!

TRANSFORMING A HOARD INTO AN ANTIQUES SHOP

Olivier initially used the property's outbuildings for storage. Then he opened his boutique Le Breuil. Arranged around a symbolic birdcage—it's a little house with trompe l'oeil brick walls—decorative objects, indoor furniture, and bibelots are displayed side by side with outdoor pieces. You might find a photo album, a perforated metal magazine rack by the French-Hungarian designer Matégot, an Egyptian goose in a glass case, Loom armchairs, and zinc and cast-iron pots and containers. Olivier admires traditional decorative flourishes and the grace of wrought-iron gazebos, but he also offers contemporary indoor—outdoor designs inspired by winter gardens. So you'll find designs by the creative duo Binôme and clean-lined zinc benches by Domani. Olivier also offers all the tools that a demanding gardener might need, as well as birdhouse essentials, and a friendly garden gnome.

A HALF-TIMBERED HIDEAWAY

The road is lined with flowers. Bordered by box trees, it leads to Maison Pelé's studio. Her feet protected by sturdy Ugg boots, Laure walks along the winding path of old Parisian cobblestones each morning. Armchairs, club and cocktail chairs, padded benches, chaises longues, and prie-dieux await her ministration in the workshop, sorely in need of repair and reupholstering. After training at the École Boulle, she started a new career as an upholsterer working out of her own house. This unexpected development was motivated by a yearning for country living. She wanted a house in the provincial countryside and a garden like the one her grandfather cultivated in Brittany. She also felt a need to live in a healthy atmosphere and offer her children the experience of an alternative way of life. She chose the woods and valleys of the French nature reserve of Vexin, tucked away between the banks of the Oise and the chalky cliffs lining the Seine. The house stands amid landscapes and villages that were beloved by the Impressionists. There's even a beach on the opposite bank, built during the 1930s, which is swept by gusts of ocean wind during long summer days. Retro-style vacation villas line the riverbanks. Her house was constructed within the foundations of a fourteenth-century farmhouse whose walls were pierced to accommodate large French windows. Laure has arranged piles of old linens, lace, and teapots in armoires. On the walls, she's hung photos of the seaside, and of Paris too—the personal memories that she cherishes privately in her winter garden.

In the living room, natural light blends with lighting from studio ceiling fixtures, which are mirrored in a trompe l'oeil photo from the vintage furniture store Carouche. The furnishings—a collection of children's chairs, an iconic Eames RAR rocking chair, and a desk discovered at decorator Gilles Jauffret's store—are tied together by a colorful antique Moldavian kilim carpet.

A chicken-wire bell jar designed by Christelle from Bord de Scène, a stack of
wooden boxes from La Brocante de la Bruyère, a display of cement mushrooms
found at Le Vide-Grenier d'une Parisienne, an oversize star procured from
The Upper Rust in New York, and Grundig Audiorama speakers bagged on eBay:
whether useful or useless, a simple decorative object or a practical piece of
furniture for storing collectibles, all the pieces are discovered, recovered,
very occasionally revamped, but more often than not left in their
original state, and always contribute to the whole.

The bedrooms are on the upper floor, behind the half-timbered house walls. Under the benevolent gaze of Alsatian storks, the children are growing up as quickly as styles are changing. At the moment, Joseph is living in a harvest-gold room. His headboard incorporates a Citroën H radiator cover and is topped with mushroom-shaped money boxes from woodworking shops in the Jura. Ten-year-old Lucien has not yet decided on the color of his bedroom walls, but he is sure he'll grow up to be a robotics engineer.

WORKING FROM HOME

In the former winter garden, a floor of Emery flower-patterned cement tiles leads out to the actual garden. The man of the house uses the space as an office. The bookcase, uncovered chez Patrick Deloison, holds a collection of travel guides, dictionaries, and model cars. Terrestrial globes are artfully grouped together, and wall maps are on display or stored away in their Vidal-Lablache case, discovered on Alicia de Rolland's stand. All reveal a pronounced taste for geographic treasures. A comfortable armchair covered in Skaï leatherette from Ring Mobblefabbrik in Norway stands by the desk. The wall clocks—from the IBM factory, Charvet-Delorme, Brillié, Simplex, Ato, and Ericsson—haven't told the right time for years. It doesn't really matter—when you work from home, you don't need to pay attention to the time.

The workshop that stands at the end of the
cobblestone path has been restored with oak window
frames like those in the main house. It is illuminated
by ceiling lights and a fixture produced by Atelier
Brutalux in homage to Jean Prouvé's celebrated
Potence wall suspension light. Matching armchairs
await reupholstering before they resume their place
back in the house, where they belong.

ACKNOWLEDGMENTS

The author offers his sincere thanks to
all the owners who opened the doors
of their homes to him.

Hélène Dufour and Jean-Pierre Richard
Un Mas à Ménerbes
Guesthouse (page 11)
84560 Ménerbes
+ 33 (0)6 11 18 19 75
www.mas-luberon.com

Modderne, design articles
www.modderne.com

Michelle and Sylvain Leredde
Au Ralenti du Lierre
Guesthouse (page 27)
Village of Les Beaumettes, 84220 Gordes
+ 33 (0)4 90 72 39 22
www.auralentidulierre.com

Thierry Dulieu and Serge Rozenweig
La Galerie du Désordre
Art and collectibles
1, Rue Vaubecour, 69002 Lyon
+ 33 (0)6 16 46 02 94
galeriedudesordre.tumblr.com

Hélène and Yannick Lafourcade
Le Clos des Trémières
Antiques shop and guesthouse (page 47)
20, Haute Rue, 49730 Montsoreau
+ 33 (0)2 41 50 72 12
www.leclosdestremieres.com

Céline and Pierre Génin
Lum'Art
Exceptional lighting fixtures (page 59)
8, Avenue du Général-de-Gaulle, 28190 Pontgouin
+ 33 (0)2 37 37 40 93
www.lumart.fr

Josiane and Joël Lenoir
L'Hôtel de Suhard
Guesthouse (page 79)
34, Rue d'Alençon, 61130 Bellême
+ 33 (0)2 33 83 53 47
www.hotel-de-suhard.fr

Grégoire Courtin
Antiques dealer and designer (page 95)
26, Rue de l'Hôtel-de-Ville, 72340 La Chartre-sur-le-Loir
+ 33 (0)6 20 62 67 17

Anne Soulier
Photographer (page 109)
www.annesoulier.com
+ 33 (0)6 10 49 61 13

Karine, François, and Nina Sédard
L'Épicerie du Pape
Guesthouse (page 127)
5, Rue de la Ferme, 27910 Vascoeuil
+ 33 (0)2 35 23 64 37
www.lepiceriedupape.com

Micheline Marchand
Les Nomades Baroques
Guesthouse (page 143)
Rue Basse, 30430 Barjac
+ 33 (0)6 24 16 68 43
www.lesnomadesbaroques.com

Chantal Guyard
Traveler (page 157)
manon21.blogspot.fr
instagram.com/manon21blog

Olivier de Vleeschouwer
Le Breuil
Collectibles and garden décor (page 169)
Route de Bonsmoulins, 61380 Moulins-la-Marche
+ 33 (0)6 63 60 58 73
www.lebreuil.pro

Laure Pelé (and Joseph and Lucien)
Maison Pelé
Furniture upholstery (page 185)
+ 33 (0)6 11 07 07 15
www.maisonpele.fr

The author would also like to thank interior
stylist Isabelle Chabeur for the photo styling in
"Château Life"; Helen Adedotun, Ryma Bouzid,
and the team at Flammarion for the creation
of this new book, with a special thank-you
to Kate Mascaro for her judicious eye.

Pages 6–7: Claude Monet's gardens in Giverny.
Pages 206–7: trees at the guesthouse
La Métairie des Bois, in Touraine.

Conception, Design, and Typesetting: Sébastien Siraudeau
www.delavolvo.fr

Translated from the French by Elizabeth Heard
Copyediting: Penelope Isaac
Proofreading: Nicole Foster
Color Separation: Quat'coul, Paris
Printed in Malaysia by Tien Wah Press

Simultaneously published in French as *À la maison*
© Flammarion, S.A., Paris, 2015

English-language edition
© Flammarion, S.A., Paris, 2015

All rights reserved.
No part of this publication may be reproduced in any form
or by any means, electronic,photocopy, information retrieval system,
or otherwise, without written permission from
Flammarion, S.A.
87, quai Panhard et Levassor
75647 Paris Cedex 13

editions.flammarion.com

15 16 17   3 2 1

ISBN: 978-2-08-020226-0

Dépôt légal: 08/2015